Learning LOL

Welcome to my class, fun facts about Places Around the World! My name is Professor Charlie, and I am so excited to show you all the fun things my assistant and I have been learning. My assistant is my mom, and she is super helpful! She reads all of the research we do together out loud, takes me for walks when it is time for a break, finds yummy treats for the both of us to share, and also does all the typing since she has fingers and thumbs, and I only have paws, and the most important thing of all, she gives the best belly rubs. My job is to give her fun ideas to look up, to keep her warm with cuddles, and to try not to bark at the mailman. I make no promises about the last one. We make a really great team!

After two days of rain, with more rain coming and being unable to go outside for walks, my assistant and I decided to do spring cleaning in our office. I was feather-dusting our bookshelves when I saw something new. It was a blue and green round ball that was on a stand. I love playing with balls and running after them! I asked my assistant if we could play with this new toy after we were done because I had been a very good boy. My mom, I mean my assistant, told me I was a super good boy and rubbed my head, but this was not a new throwing and chasing toy. It was something called a "globe," and we could learn about these different places called 'countries' around the world. I was a little disappointed that I didn't get a new ball to play with, but I was excited to learn about this "globe" and what countries were.

After we were all done cleaning, my assistant and I got a yummy snack (peanut butter & apples, our favorite!), sat on our favorite comfy sofa by the window, and enjoyed our treats. We both love listening to the sound of the rain hitting the window. I asked her if we could look at the "globe" now, and she said yes! She got the blue and green ball off the shelf and asked me to please bring her laptop. I quickly jumped up from the sofa, gently got my assistant's laptop for her, and placed it on the couch. Once we were both snuggled back on the sofa, she told me to spin the globe around. She said that all of the green places were where people in the world lived, and the blue places were all water. My assistant explained that we all live on Earth, and billions of people live here in different

environments, speaking different languages and eating different kinds of foods. I was shocked by this! I saw many people when we went on walks, but I never thought some people spoke different languages and lived differently than we did. I then started asking her so many questions. She smiled, patted my head, and told me about the different continents, counties, provinces, states, and cities. I learned that I live in a country called the United States of America and in the state of Michigan. We have big lakes around the state.

My tail started wagging uncontrollably because I was so excited to see all these new places and try new yummy food. I wonder what flavor of dog bones they will have? I told my assistant we needed to visit all these places and I could start packing our suitcases. She laughed and smiled, saying that it would be so much fun to travel to these new places, but very expensive to go to every place in the world, but we could travel for free on the computer. So that is what we did! I pointed to a place on the "globe," and she found pictures for us to look at and videos for us to watch.

After learning about so many amazing places, I told my assistant that we needed to share these places with our pup pals, so that's what we did. We found some fun facts about the cool places we learned about and wrote this book for you. Did you know that some places have buildings that are thousands of years old? I also saw a giant hole in the ground that used to be an ocean! I never knew that the world around me was so big and amazing. Please don't worry if you don't understand something that I wrote because I made sure everything was super easy to look up if you didn't understand. Looking up things you don't know is a wonderful way for you to learn how to be a researcher, like me! But please ask an adult if it is ok to use the computer before you begin your research. Manners and safety first! I hope you enjoy our book, our new pup pal. We will see you for your next lesson!

Tara & Charlie Morrish

Photos by: Scarlet Morrish

Professor Charlie   Smokey

Learning LOL

Where learning language online is fun!

We want to thank you, from the bottom of our paws to the tips of our ears, for buying our book! We hope you enjoyed reading it as much as we enjoyed writing and researching it. We are also excited to share that you can join us on our website soon. Here, you can view your favorite topics with videos, maps, pictures, interactive worksheets, and flashcards. Scan the QR code to make entering the classroom easier, but remember to ask your grown-up before going online. See you there!

Have fun learning online!   *Have fun learning with more books!*

Learninglol.com

Maps

Time Zones

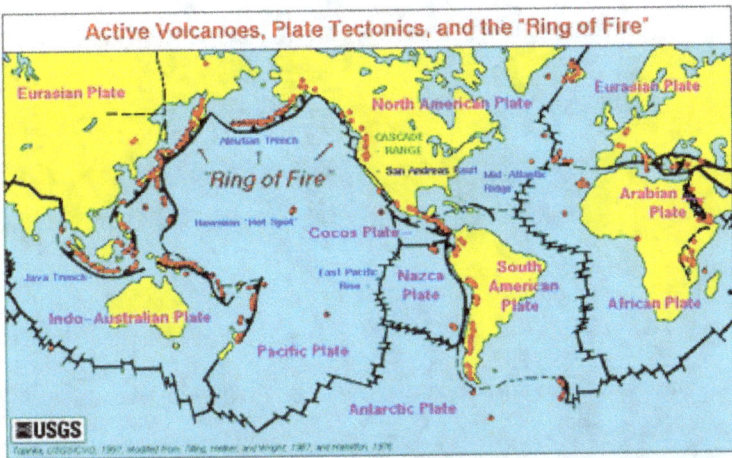

World Topography

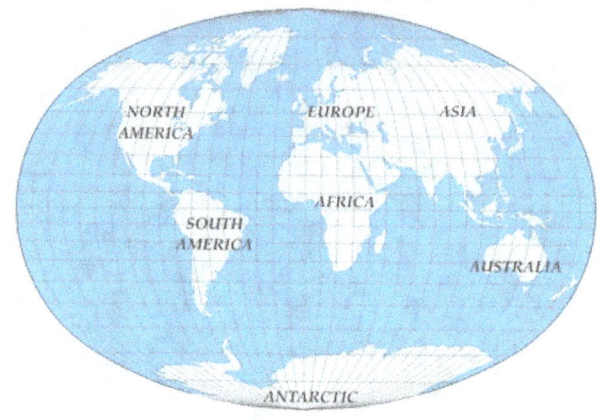

7 Continents

Climate Zones, Scenario B2 2001 - 2025, Global
National Aggregates of Geospatial Data Collection

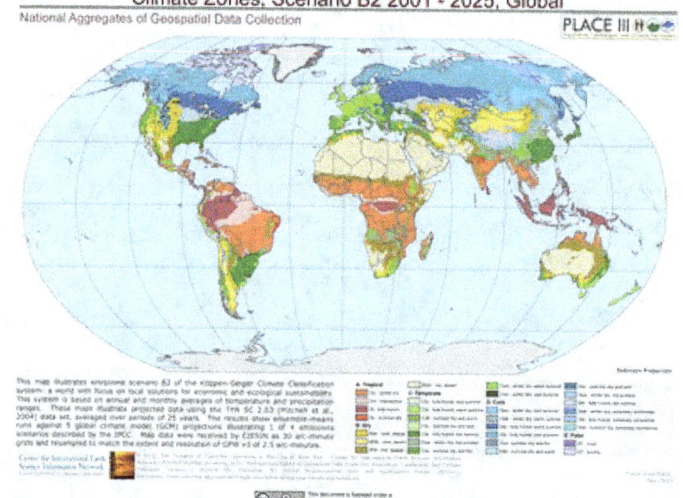

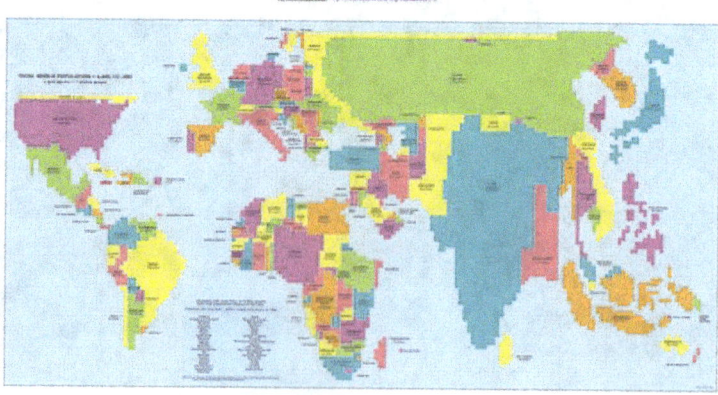

The country size is shown as population size (1 grid square 1 million people)

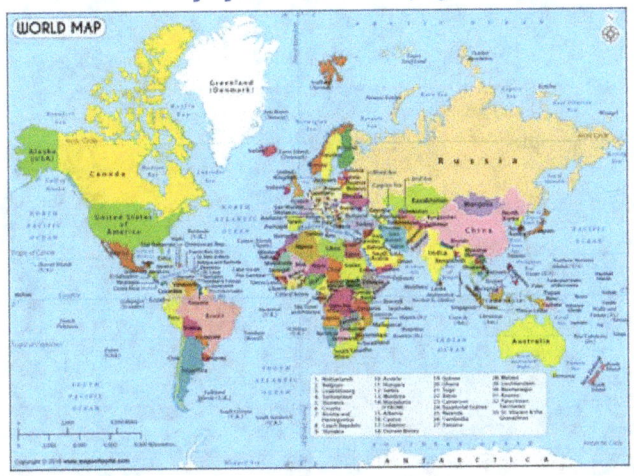

ALL WORLD FLAGS

Where learning language online is fun!

Learning About the World Around Us!

Table of Contents

Learning About the World Around Us!

Angkor Wat

★**Location**: **Siem Reap, Cambodia (Continent of Asia)**

★**Built by:** Built by Khmer Emperor Suryavarman II

★**How long to build**: It took about 34 years to build

★**Date built**: During the early 1100s, it was the capital of the empire (about 920 years ago)

★**Size**: It spans around 400 acres (1.6 km²)

★**Weight**: Made with 5-10 million sandstone blocks, each weighing about 1.5 tons (1.4 metric tons)

★First built as a Hindu temple dedicated to the god Vishnu (for about 100 years), it was conquered after a war and turned into a Buddhist temple.

★It is said that 300,000 laborers and 6,000 elephants helped build the complex.

★Surrounding Angkor Wat, a massive moat is 650 ft (200 m) wide and 13 ft (4 m) deep.

★The temple's five tower peaks are supposed to represent Mount Meru, the home of the gods, in both Hindu and Buddhist faiths. The walls and moat honor the surrounding mountain ranges and the sea.

★By the late 1400s, the population of the complex slowly declined because of war, drought, and new trading opportunities with other countries.

Learning About the World Around Us!

★There is some evidence that the original purpose was as a burial tomb for Emperor Suryavarman II because of the way the building is facing, and it is facing West. In the Hindu religion, funerary temples always face the West. All other temples face the East. But, there was no evidence of Emperor Suryavarman II in the tomb.

★Throughout the temple, there are beautiful stone carvings of 8 Hindu stories and carvings of Buddha.

★Angkor Wat is a significant symbol of Cambodia, and it is on the country's money and flag, among countless products.

Where learning language online is fun!

Learning About the World Around Us!

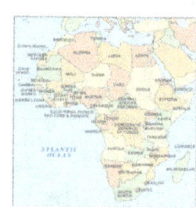

Boulders Beach

★<u>Location</u>: Simon's Town (south of Cape Town), South Africa (Continent of Africa)

★<u>What's interesting here?</u> There is an African penguin colony that lives here, and you can get up close to them

★<u>How many are there?</u> Today, there are about 3,000 of them

★<u>Date they arrived</u>: In 1982, two pairs (4 penguins) of penguins arrived in False Bay (the body of water the beach is at) and started the colony

★Their numbers are decreasing, and they are on the Endangered list because their habitat is becoming smaller, and there is insufficient food and pollution. So today, the beach is protected by law to help their numbers hopefully recover.

★You can go and see them, but you must keep your distance and can not feed them. There is a fee (money) to enter. There is a boardwalk that goes out to the beach, where you can go and see the penguins.

★You can swim here, but it is at a different part of the beach than the boardwalk. You may meet a penguin friend but don't touch if one swims up to you.

★About African Penguins★

★<u>Animal class</u>: Birds (Have feathers, a beak (no teeth), two legs, two wings (some species cannot fly), have vertebrae (spine or backbone), are warm-blooded (the body temperature stays about the same temperature),

Learning About the World Around Us!

lay eggs, might be related to dinosaurs, have a four-chamber heart (4 parts), most have excellent eyesight and range in size from the **Bee hummingbird** at 2.2 in (5.5 cm) to the **Ostrich** at 9 ft (3 m) tall)

(Examples: Penguins, parrots, owls, and hawks) There are around 11,000 different species)

★**Diet**: **Carnivores (They only eat meat)**: small fish, crabs, shrimp, and squid

★**Lifespan**: About 15-20 years

★**Predators**: Sharks, mongooses, seals, cats, and birds

★**Size**: About 2 ft (61 cm) tall

★**Speed**: They can swim about 15 mph (24 kmh) when they are hunting

★**Weight**: About 8 lb (4 kg)

Where learning language online is fun!

Learning About the World Around Us!

The Burj Khalifa

★**Location**: Dubai, United Arab Emirates (Continent of Asia and the Middle East region)

★**Built by:** Designed by American architect Adrian Smith

★**How long to build**: It took 6 years to build

★**Date built**: It opened in 2010

★**Size**: It is the world's tallest building at 2,717 ft (828 m) tall

★**Weight**: About 450,000 tons (460,000 metric tons). The weight is about the same as 100,000 elephants!

★It holds world records!!
  1. The tallest freestanding structure
  2. The highest number of floors- 200 floors
  3. The highest occupied floor- 160 floors where people live and work
  4. The highest outdoor observation deck- Floor 148 (1,821 ft or 555 m above the ground)
  5. The elevator with the longest travel distance- 1,653 ft (504 m) going up
  6. The highest restaurant- Floor 122 (1,447 ft or 441 m above the ground)

★ There are 900 homes, office suites, Armani Hotel and Residences (144 residences), an observation deck, supermarkets, fancy restaurants, shops,

Learning About the World Around Us!

swimming pools, lounges, and a four-story health club.

★ At the base of the building are six giant water fountains, colorful trees, and beautiful green gardens.

★To clean all of the windows outside the building takes about three months.

★This building is very environmentally friendly! It has about 340 solar panels to help heat the water for the building, and it recycles water from the air conditioning system to help water the trees, plants, and flowers around the building. It provides 15 million gallons of water annually or 20 Olympic-sized swimming pools.

★If you look at the Burj Khalifa from the top, you can see a flower design. The architect based the design on a popular desert flower called a "Spider lily." You can also see a lot of Islamic influence in the design.

★In 2021, Emirates Airlines filmed a commercial where a flight attendant stood on top of the building.

View from the observation deck on the 148 floor

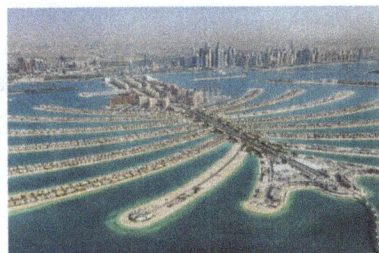

Dubai's Palm shaped island, Palm Jumeirah

Spider lily flower

Learning About the World Around Us!

Christist the Redeemer

★**Location**: Rio de Janeiro, Brazil, on Mount Corcovado (Continent of South America)

★**Built by:** Brazilian engineer Heitor da Silva Costa designed the statue with the help of French sculptor Paul Landowski

★**How long to build**: It took nine years to build

★**Date built**: Construction started in 1922, and in 1931, the statue construction completed

★**Size**: The statue is 98 ft (30 m) tall and has an arm span of 92 ft (28 m)

★**Weight:** The concrete and soapstone tiles weigh about 1,400,000 lbs (635 tons)

★It is a statue of Jesus Christ, symbolizing the loving embrace of Christ.

★Mount Corcovado is 2,310 ft (704 m) high, and the statue sits at its peak. The statue is visible for miles (kilometers) throughout the city below.

★The statue is slowly changing color because it uses different materials and needs repair. The original materials are rare now.

★ Workers in France built part of the statue, and then it was shipped over the ocean to Brazil, where it was put back together and reinforced.

★Over the years, the statue has been through a lot of rough weather. It has been struck by lightning many times, and once, lightning took off one of the tips of the statue's fingers.

Learning About the World Around Us!

★Before 2003, you had to climb 200 steps to visit it in person. Now, there are escalators and elevators for a more leisurely visit.

★About 2 million people visit annually. At the base of the statue are a small restaurant and a chapel for visitors to enjoy.

★When the statue needs repair, workers must tie themselves to a rope and repel down to the statue that needs repair. They will even walk on the arms to help fix the hands.

Worker repairing the statue.

Learning About the World Around Us!

The Colosseum

★**Location**: **Rome, Italy** **(Continent of Europe)**

★**Built by:** Emperor Vespasian as a gift to the Roman people

★**Date built**: Construction started in 70 AD and finished in 80 AD (about 2,000 years ago)

★**How long to build**: It took ten years to build

★**Size**: 620 ft long & 513 ft wide & 158 ft tall (190 m long & 155 m wide & 48 m tall)

★**Weight**: 245 million lbs (295,000 m tons)

★With the completion of the Colosseum, the current Emperor Titus (the son of Emperor Vespasian) held 100 days of games, including gladiatorial combats and wild animal fights for the people.

★The Colosseum had seating for more than 50,000 spectators, and on hot days, there was an awning to help protect the people from the sun.

★About 60,000 to 100,000 Jewish enslaved people built the Colosseum.

★It is the largest ancient amphitheater ever built, and you can still visit.

★One use for the Colosseum was for gladiator fights with wild animals, such as lions, tigers, hippos, bears, elephants, giraffes, and rhinos.

★Gladiators were made up of men and a few women who were criminals,

Learning About the World Around Us!

enslaved people, prisoners of war, and people who wanted to fight for fame and glory.

★They would also flood the arena to have mock (fake) naval engagements.

★Around the arena, workers would open different trap doors (36 trap doors in total) for releasing wild animals into the arena and for special effects during a performance.

★There were also tunnels and rooms under the floor of the arena. These tunnels are where they would keep the animals and the gladiators and performers coming and going in the Colosseum.

★In about 400 years, about 400,000 people died fighting in the arena, and about 1 million animals died.

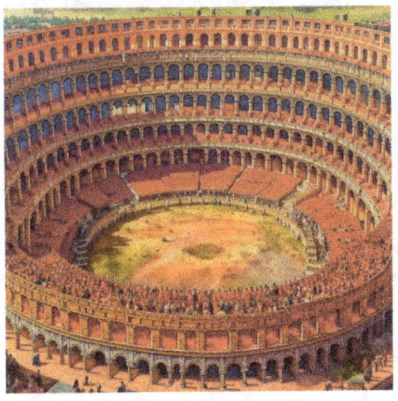

Naval Battle

Where learning language online is fun!

Learning About the World Around Us!

Easter Island or Rapa Nui

★<u>Location</u>: **A remote Island 2,300 mi (3,700 km) off the coast of Chile** (**Continent of South America**)

★<u>Built by:</u> Rapa Nui (the native people of the island)

★<u>How long to build</u>: Each Moai statue could take up to 2 years to crave

★<u>Date built</u>: Between the years 1400-1650

★<u>Size</u>: They are about 13 ft (4 m) tall and 5.5 ft (1.6 m) wide

★<u>Weight</u>: They weigh about 27,500 lb (12.5 tons) (about two elephants)

★The Moai (the big heads)represent the faces of ancestors who help protect the island and its people.

★All of the statues have bodies, but some of the bodies are partially underground.

★There are about 900 Moai on Easter Island, made from the rocks of the island's volcanoes. They used handheld chisels made out of durable stones.

★Some statues still have the "pukao" (red hats), representing the topknot hair bun that the Rapa Nui wore. All high-ranking men never cut their hair and wore it in a top knot. They did this because they believed their hair was connected to spiritual power.

Learning About the World Around Us!

★The island was made by three volcanoes between 100,000 and 3 million years ago; they are all dormant (inactive) now. There is a lake in the creator of one of the volcanos.

★The first people were said to have arrived on the island between 700 and 800 AD (about 1,100 and 1,200 years ago).

★There are about 8,000 people who currently live on the island.

★The only way to get here is a 5-7 hour plane ride (depending on the city your plane leaves). There are no harbors for boats.

★In 1722, Dutch explorer Jacob Roggeveen was the first European to land on the island, naming it "Easter Island."

Learning About the World Around Us!

The Eiffel Tower

★<u>Location</u>: Paris, France   (Continent of Europe)

★<u>Built by:</u> Alexandre Gustave Eiffel didn't design this tower even though it has his name. Two of his employees, two structural engineers named Maurice Koechlin and Emile Nouguier, came up with the design of the Eiffel Tower.

★<u>Date built</u>: It was built for the 1889 World's Fair to mark the 100th anniversary of the French Revolution (a war in France). (almost 135 years ago)

★<u>How long to build</u>: The Tower was finished in record time, two years, two months, and five days.

★<u>Size</u>: It is 1,063 ft (324 m) tall

★<u>Weight</u>: 22,300,000 lbs (10,100 tons), about the same as 95 blue whales

★There is a private apartment at the top! Eiffel and other scientists used this apartment to live in sometimes and used it as a laboratory for weather and radio experiments. He would invite extraordinary people like Thomas Edison into the apartment. Now it is a museum, and you can look inside.

★The 1st floor has museum exhibits, a glass floor, changing exhibitions, a souvenir shop, and a restaurant. The 2nd floor has the Jules Verne restaurant and an observation area. The 3rd floor has an observation area and a drink stand.

Learning About the World Around Us!

★Also, on the first floor, there is a small post office where you can send a letter, and there will be a special postmark you can only get here.

★ The tower also has 72 names engraved on it of French scientists, engineers, and mathematicians who made significant contributions in their fields.

★ Under the tower is an old military bunker (underground rooms) used in 1914 during WWI to help send radio signals to French troops. Today, the tower houses a small museum and food preparation rooms for the restaurants.

City View

Alexandre Eiffel (right), his daughter Claire (center), and Thomas Edison (left).

Names of some of the important French contributors

Where learning language online is fun!

Learning About the World Around Us!

The Elizabeth Tower

(Big Ben is the name of the largest bell inside the tower)

★<u>Location</u>: Westminster, London, (United Kingdom) (Continent of Europe)

★<u>Built by:</u> Architects Charles Barry and Augustus Welby Pugin

★<u>Date built</u>: Constructed in 1367, it was the first tower and clock. In 1698, the tower was torn down and rebuilt with a sundial instead of a clock. In 1859, after a fire had burned the Palace of Westminster, another tower and clock were built (about 66 years ago).

★<u>How long to build</u>: It took 13 years to build

★<u>Size</u>: 315 ft (96 m) tall. The tower has 11 floors, 334 steps to the bells, and another 55 stairs to get to the light at the top. They light it when Parliament (England's government) is in session.

★<u>Weight</u>: The bell (Big Ben, the largest bell in the tower) weighs about 14 tons (14,225 kg)

★The Palace of Westminster used to be a royal residence, but now it is the meeting place for both the House of Commons and the House of Lords, the two houses of the Parliament of the United Kingdom.

★Big Ben is only a nickname for the tower. The actual name is Elizabeth Tower (dedicated to the queen in 2012 for her 60 years on the throne). It used to be called The Clock Tower.

★There are five bells, each between 1.2-4 tons (1,219-4,064 kg).

Learning About the World Around Us!

★ Four clocks on the tower keep time very accurate. Each week, the clocks are wound three times and are only about 2 seconds off. To help keep the best time, they will put an English penny on or off the pendulums (they part in the clock that swings).

★ The name of the great bell is under debate. Some say the name came from the First Commissioner for Works, Sir Benjamin Hall, and others say the name came from the bare-knuckle heavyweight boxing champion Ben Caunt.

Palace of Westminster

Big Ben

Benjamin Caunt

Workers making repairs.

Where learning language online is fun!

Learning About the World Around Us!

Giant's Causeway

★**Location**: **Northern Ireland (United Kingdom) (Continent of Europe)**

★**Created by:** Formed by volcanic eruptions, the lava flows slowly to the sea and cools down. The hardened lava cracked and formed the pillars when after it cooled.

★**Date created**: 50 to 60 million years ago

★**Size**: 4 mi (6 km) along the northern coast. The pillars are about 15-20 inches (38-51 cm) in diameter (around) and up to 82 feet (25 m) in height. There are also pillars on nearby cliffs, which can be 330 ft (100 m) in height

★There are about 40,000 of these basalt pillars, most of which have six sides, but some have 5-to 8 sides.

★Around 2011, geologists (a person who studies the Earth) found stromatolites (rock-like structures made by bacteria called blue-green algae) in the colder water of Ireland. People can find these structures in warm water, so it was a significant find (this bacteria acts as a plant because it uses photosynthesis).

★There are about 50 different species of birds that make their homes here, so if you like to bird-watch, you will see shags, redshanks, and the razorbill, to name just a few.

★Over 300,000 visitors go to the Giants Causeway each year, climb on the rocks, hike along the coast, and explore nearby caves.

Learning About the World Around Us!

★**There is an old myth:** A giant called Finn McCool from Ireland was trying to protect his homeland from a Scottish giant named Benandonner. The Scottish giant was trying to take the island of Ireland for himself. To help protect the island, McCool threw huge rocks and hurled them into the water, forming a bridge (causeway) so he could go to Scotland and defeat Benandonner. Once McCool got to Scotland, he realized he was much smaller than Benandonner, so he needed a new idea. McCool ran back to Ireland and dressed up like a baby to fool Benandonner into thinking the babies of Ireland were the size of a small giant. When Benandonner crossed the causeway, he was the "baby" McCool and got scared because if the baby was that big, his father must be enormous. Benandonner raced back to Scotland, and on his way back, he destroyed the bridge so McCool could not come after him. This myth is why you can find the basalt pillars in Ireland and Scotland.

The "boot" of Fin McCool.

Where learning language online is fun!

Learning About the World Around Us!

The Grand Canyon

★<u>Location</u>: **Arizona, U.S.A** **(Continent of North America)**

★<u>Date created:</u> The Colorado River flowed through it for over 6 million years, carving out the canyon

★<u>Size</u>: In some areas, it is up to 18 mi (29 km) wide & 1 mi (1.6 km) deep along its 277 mi (446 km) length

★Layered bands of colorful rock reveal years of geologic history throughout the canyon.

★It became a national park in 1919.

★Supai Village, the capital of the Havasupai Indian Reservation, has a population of a hundred residents. You must walk there 8 mi (12 km) or fly in by helicopter. You can also find Havasupai Falls in this area.

★It is the most remote community in the continental United States, and the mule delivers and carries out mail.

★There are more than 1,000 caves in the canyon made over the years by water. You can take cave tours through some of them.

★There are many trails that you can hike, but make sure you make the proper preparations.

★They have found fossils in the canyon, but not dinosaur fossils. They have found plant-like animals, shells, coral, sponges, dragonfly wing imprints, and more.

Learning About the World Around Us!

★The canyon was once under the ocean between 740 million to 1.2 billion years ago.

★Human artifacts have been found from about 12,000 years ago, from when people first started living in the canyon.

★There is a glass horseshoe bridge that will take you about 70 ft (22 m) over the canyon rim so you can look over the edge. You can visit the bridge in the western part of the Grand Canyon.

..Sup ai Village.

Havasupai Falls

Learning About the World Around Us!

The Great Barrier Reef

★**Location**: **Queensland, Australia (off the coast) (Continent of Australia)**

★**Date created**: Created over 20 million years ago. When old coral dies, new coral will grow on top of it, so it never stops growing

★**Size**: It is about 1,429 mi (2,300 km) long and 40 mi (65 km) wide & It is 82 ft (35 m) deep close to shore and 1.5 mi (2,000 m) on the outer reef

★Parts of the ocean floor the reefs are on were once dry land about 10,000 years ago, at the end of the Ice Age. When the glaciers started to melt, their waters flooded the area.

★The world's most extensive coral reef system comprises over 2,900 individual reefs and 900 islands.

★10% of the world's fish inhabit (live in or around) the Great Barrier Reef.

★It can be seen from space because it is so big!

★The reef is the largest living structure made of animals on Earth.

★Coral is not a type of plant. They are animals. There are about 600 different species that help make up the reef.

★There are more than 30 species of whale, dolphin, and porpoise, 6 species of sharks, 6 species of turtle, 17 species of sea snake, 100 species of jellyfish, 220 species of birds, and more than 1,500 species of fish.

Learning LOL

Learning About the World Around Us!

★You can go scuba diving in parts of the reef. Just be careful of the sharks.

View from above

Butterflyfish & Coral

Sea Turtle

Yellow-bellied snake

Australian Pied Oystercatcher

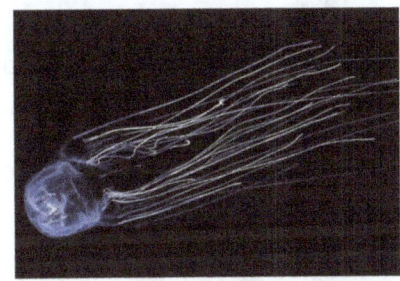

Box jellyfish

Tiger shark

Porpoise

Where learning language online is fun!

Learning About the World Around Us!

The Great Pyramid of Giza

★<u>Location</u>: Giza, Egypt (Continent of Africa)

★<u>Built by:</u> Pharaoh Khufu for his tomb (He was the 2nd pharaoh of the 4th Dynasty)

★<u>Date built</u>: 2589-2566 BCE (about 4,500 years ago)

★<u>How long to build</u>: It took about 22 years to build

★<u>Size</u>: It is 479 ft (146 m) tall and is the tallest of the three pyramids in the complex

★<u>Weight</u>: It took over 2 million stones. It weighs about 5.75 million tons in total. Each block weighs about 2.3 metric tons (2267.96 kg)

★Archaeologists think the workers used ramps wrapped around the sides as they built the pyramid.

★On the outside of the Great Pyramid, there used to be white limestone, which made the side smooth, and on the top, there was a gold cap.

★The people who built the pyramid were mainly paid workers who were well cared for and fed. Some enslaved people helped build the pyramid, but not as many as archaeologists had previously thought.

★The other smaller pyramids at Giza are the Pyramid of Khafre (the son of Khufu) and the Pyramid of Menkaure (the son of Khafre and the grandson of Khufu). The three smaller pyramids at Giza go with Pharaoh

Learning About the World Around Us!

Menkaure's pyramid. But none of them seem to have been completed. They found one empty sarcophagus in one. The other two were empty, but some paintings were on the walls.

★It was one of the original seven wonders of the ancient world, and only one still stands the Great Pyramid. The seven wonders of the ancient world were The statue of Zeus at Olympia, The Colossus of Rhodes, the Hanging Gardens of Babylon, the Great Pyramid of Giza, the Temple of Artemis at Ephesus, the Mausoleum at Halicarnassus, and the Lighthouse of Alexandria.

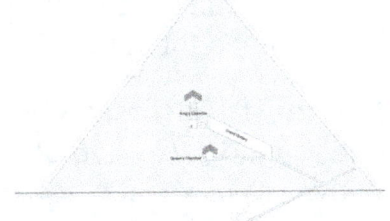

Inside the Grand Gallery

Granite coffer of the Pharaoh Khufu

Old 7 Wonders of the World

New 7 Wonders of the World

Where learning language online is fun!

Learning About the World Around Us!

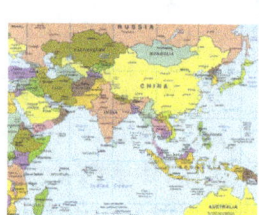 

The Great Wall of China

★<u>Location</u>: Huairou District, China (Continent of Asia)

★<u>Built by:</u> Many different dynasties built different sections of the wall and then joined them together

★<u>Date built</u>: The first section started in the state of Chu; construction started around 770 – 476 BC during the Spring and Autumn Period (the Zhou dynasty). (about 2,700 years ago)

★<u>How long to build</u>: It took over 2,000 years to build The Great Wall of China throughout all the different dynasties (the individual Warring States, Qin, Han, and Ming dynasties)

★<u>Weight</u>: About 3,873,000,000 individual bricks and about 100,000,000 tonnes of stone, bricks, and mud make up the Great Wall.

★<u>Size</u>: The length is 13,170 mi (21,196 km)

★The wall started as individual walls and watchtowers that protected small kingdoms that the Mongols from the north were invading.

★Emperor Qin Shi Huang (259 - 210 BC) ordered that the northern sections of the wall and each state's borders join to form a unified line of defense against Mongol harassment from the north, the first actual Great Wall.

★The workers used sticky rice to hold the stones together.

Learning About the World Around Us!

★The workers were primarily prisoners, but soldiers and the poor helped build the wall. Prisoners had to shave their heads, blacken their faces, and wear chains around their feet.

★About 400,000 people died building the Great Wall.

★When a person died during this time, their family would come to the wall and carry a rooster over the wall where they died. They believed the rooster's crowing would help their spirit from being trapped in the wall and walk it forever.

★The People's Republic of China has been rebuilding parts of the wall since about 1957.

★About ⅓ of the original wall has disappeared over time due to time and weather.

★ Today, it is one of the "7 Wonders of the World" and is the longest artificial structure.

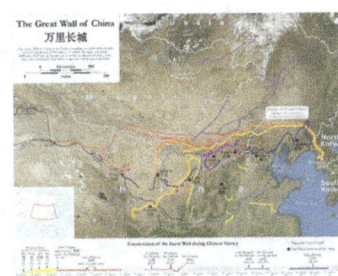

Sticky rice holding the bricks together.

Emperor Qin Shi Huang.

Learning About the World Around Us!

Lake Hillier

★<u>Location</u>: **It's on the Middle Island near Southwestern Australia** **(Continent of Australia)**

★<u>Created by</u>: Algae and bacteria cause the lake to have a pink color

★<u>Size</u>: It is about 2,000 ft (600 m) long, about 820 ft (250 m) wide, and it is a shallow lake, just a few feet (meters) depending on the rainfall and the ocean levels

★There is about ten times more salt in the lake than in the ocean, and a layer of dried salt surrounds the lake's edge.

★The only animals that live in the lake are micro-organisms such as different-colored algae and bacteria because they can survive high salt levels. Research by scientists shows that the algae and bacteria reacting with the high salt levels cause the pink color of the water in the lake.

★It has eucalyptus and paperbark trees along the coast to separate it from the ocean.

★It was found in 1802 by Mathew Flinders, a British Navigator and Cartographer, and he named the lake after a crewmate named William Hillier, who fell sick and died.

★In the late 1880s, a father and sons tried to mine the lake to access the salt, but shortly after production started, they realized the salt was not good for food and shut down production.

Learning About the World Around Us!

★It is safe to swim in the lake, but it is not allowed. It is now protected land under the government.

★To get to Lake Hillier, the most common way is by helicopter. There are tours, but you can get there by boat. It is on a remote part of the island.

Paperbark tree

Eucalyptus tree and Koala

The Leaning Tower of Pisa

★**Location**: **Pisa, Italy** **(Continent of Europe)**

★**Built by:** There is little record of who built the tower, but a wealthy local widow (a woman whose husband has died) donated 60 silver coins in her Will (a document the person leaves after they die to tell others what to do with their stuff and money) to the church, and the following year construction started

★**Date built**: (About 849 years ago) Construction of the Tower of Pisa began in 1173, and the tower competition was in 1399 (there were many civil wars, and they had to stop building many times).

★**How long to build**: In total, it took about 226 years to complete

★**Size**: Original height: 197 ft (60 m) & today, the tallest side is 187 ft (57 m) & the lower side is 184 ft (56 m)

★**Weight**: About 14,600 tonnes

★It is the freestanding bell tower of the Cathedral of Pisa (church).

★The tower has about 294 steps to get to the top.

★At the top of the tower, there are seven bells. Each bell makes a musical note on the Major scale. The bells do not ring anymore because they may cause more damage to the tower.

Learning About the World Around Us!

★Known worldwide for its nearly four-degree lean, resulting from an unstable foundation. The land was very marshy (too much water in the grass), which caused an unstable foundation.

★Galileo (a famous scientist who was an astronomer, physicist, and engineer) was baptized (to be blessed by God) in the baptistery (a small building outside the church) in 1565.

★Engineers have improved the tower over the years to help save it. They say it will be stable for about 200 years unless there is some kind of natural disaster like an earthquake.

...............Cathedral of Pisa................

.................Baptistery................

Tower of Pisa

Learning About the World Around Us!

The Louvre

★**Location**: **Paris, France** **(Continent of Europe)**

★**Built by:** King Phillip II (built the fort), King Francis (turned into a palace), and the National Assembly (government at the time)

★**Date built**: In the 1100s, the Louvre first served as a fortress, then a royal palace for French kings, and finally an art museum (about 930 years ago)

★**How long to build**: About 200 years, but built in different stages, starting as a fortress and now a museum

★**Size**: 652,300 sq ft (60,600 sq m) in total area

★**Weight**: The glass pyramid weighs about 200 tons (180 m tons)

★The museum started in the 1100s as a fortress to help defend against northern invaders, and after 200 years was abandoned. The first King of France, Phillip II, built it.

★In the mid-1500s, King Francis I constructed the royal fortress palace

★In 1661, King Louis XVI moved his residence to Versailles.

★After the royal residence was closed and moved from the Louvre, artists, writers, poets, and sculptors used the building for their art in the still open parts.

★In 1793, it turned into a museum.

Learning About the World Around Us!

★In 1516, Leonardo Di Vinci came to live at the royal palace at the invitation of King Francis I, who had given Di Vinci the title of "The King's First Painter, Engineer, and Architect." He died in 1519. Today, there are over 130 pieces of his work, including paintings, sculptures, drawings, notebooks, and more.

★The pyramid is 79 ft (21 m) high and is made out of 118 glass triangles, the entrance of which opened in March 1989, symbolically the bicentenary year (200 years after) of the French Revolution.

★It is estimated that it would take a person 100 days at least to see all the works of art.

★There are about 35,000 different exhibits throughout the museum.

Mona Lisa

The Wedding at Cana

Winged Victory of Samothrace

Replica of the fortress from the 1100s

Part of the original fortress

Learning About the World Around Us!

Machu Picchu

★<u>Location</u>: **Peru (in the Andes Mountains) (Continent of South America)**

★<u>Built by:</u> The Inca (a native civilization to South America)

★<u>Date built</u>: Built around 1420 (about 600 years ago)

★<u>How long to build</u>: It took about 30 years to build

★<u>Size</u>: About 1,740 ft (530 m) long by 660 ft (200 m) wide

★<u>Weight</u>: Built with stones that weighed up to 50 lbs-55 tons (23 kg-45 m tons)

★Archeologists believed it had been a royal estate or a sacred religious site for the Inca leaders. There was a population of about 1,000 people.

★It has about 180 buildings: royal houses, baths, workers' houses, temples, and sanctuaries.

★The city was built of stone without the help of wheels or iron tools, and there is no mortar (something to stick the stones together) between them because of how well they fit together.

★The buildings were also built to withstand earthquakes; two fault lines meet here. They did this knowing there were fault lines because it would have a good water supply from when it rained or melted snow, run down the sides of the mountain, and have easy access to building materials because the stones would be loose from earlier earthquakes.

Learning About the World Around Us!

★Machu Picchu was an astronomical observatory where they kept track of the moon, stars, and sun. They depended on this knowledge to understand the changing seasons, when to plant and harvest their crops, and for religious ceremonies.

★Spanish invaders wiped out most of the Inca's cities in the 16th century, but since Machu Picchu was well hidden in the mountains, they did not find it.

★ There are a lot of different animals also live on the mountain, like the Spectacled bear (the only bear in South America), alpacas, llamas, Andean Cock-of-the-Rock, pumas, Andean condor, and many different kinds of insects, mammals, and reptiles, birds.

★There are only two ways to get there today: train (2-4 hours travel depending on where you get on) or foot (4-day hike).

Spectacled bear   **Andean Cock-of-the-Rock**   **Alpacas**   **Llamas**

Learning About the World Around Us!

The Matterhorn

★<u>Location</u>: **Switzerland and Italy (on the border in the Alps Mountains) (Continent of Europe)**

★<u>Date created</u>: About 50-60 million years ago by the African and Eurasian tectonic plates

★<u>Size</u>: It is 14,692 ft (4,478 m) tall (Mt Everest is 29,032 ft (8,849 m) and is the world's tallest)

★It is one of the most recognized mountains in Europe because it is an almost perfect pyramid shape, and it is the 12th tallest mountain in Europe.

★Each side of the peak of the mountain faces the cardinal directions (North, South, East, West)

★On the 14th of July 1865, Edward Whymper and his team were the first people to have ever completed the climb to the top of the Matterhorn after others had made several unsuccessful attempts. Seven men went up the mountain for that first climb, but only three returned. The four men died after a rope broke on their way back down the mountain.

★At the summit is a metal cross to remember the estimated 500 people who have lost their lives trying to climb this mountain.

★On July 14th, 2015, the 150th anniversary of the first successful climb, they closed the mountain for climbing for the day and placed solar lights

Learning About the World Around Us!

along the path that the first climbers took. The light along the path was white except where the four climbers lost their lives

★There is an igloo resort, Iglu-Dorf Zermatt, at the mountain's base. You can rent a room!

★The oldest person to have climbed the mountain was 89-year-old Ulrich Inderbinen.

★About 3,000 people climb the Matterhorn every year.

Edward Whymper and the path he and his team took

...Iglu-Dorf Zermatt...

Where learning language online is fun!

Learning About the World Around Us!

Mount Rushmore

★**Location**: **Keystone, South Dakota, U.S.A. (Continent of North America)**

★**Built by:** Sculptor Gutzon Borglum, and after his death in 1941, his son Lincoln finished the project

★**Date built**: Construction was from 1927 to 1941 (about 81 years ago)

★**How long to build:** It took 14 years to build, and about 400 men worked on the sculptures

★**Size**: Each face is about 60 ft (18 m) high

★**Weight**: About 600 million lbs (272,155,422 million kg)

★They made the monument to attract tourists to the state of South Dakota. Today, nearly 3 million people visit every year.

★The mountain was named after a New York lawyer named Charles E. Rushmore, who came to the area to check properties and mining claims while working for a mining company. Rushmore joked about having a mountain named after him to a local guide, and the guide said they never really had a name for it, and from then on, it was called Mount Rushmore.

★The faces depict U.S. presidents George Washington, Thomas Jefferson, Theodore Roosevelt, and Abraham Lincoln.

★**George Washington** (1789–1797, 1st president) was again Commander and Chief of the army during the American Revolutionary War. England was the head of the committee that wrote the constitution and is called the "Father of His Country."

Learning About the World Around Us!

★**<u>Thomas Jefferson</u>** (1801–1809, 3rd president) signed the Louisiana Purchase, which gave the US most of its southern and middle territories, and wrote the Declaration of Independence.

★**<u>Abraham Lincoln</u>** (1861–1865, 16th president) led the country through the American Civil War and issued the Emancipation Proclamation (freeing the enslaved people).

★**<u>Theodore Roosevelt</u>** (1901-1909, 26th president) helped construct the Panama Canal, dedicated about 200 million acres of land to the National Parks, and won the Nobel Peace Prize in 1906 for helping negotiate the Russo-Japanese War (1904-1905 war between Russia and Japan).

★The monument was carved into the side of a mountain called "The Six Grandfathers." The land once belonged to the Lakota Sioux Tribe (A Native American group in the US). The tribe lost the mountain after the US government broke a treaty with them in 1877 (signed in 1868 between the two groups) after the government found gold there. The gold led to two famous battles between the Native Americans and the US Government, "Battle of Little Bighorn" (Jun 25, 1876) and "Wounded Knee." (December 29, 1890)

Workers carving and working on the monument.

Actual picture from the aftermath of the "Wounded Knee."

Where learning language online is fun!

Learning About the World Around Us!

Niagara Falls

★**Location**: **Niagara Falls, New York, U.S.A. (bordering Canada and the United States)** **(Continent of North America)**

★**Built by:** Created by large glaciers that started to melt, and the water carved out the falls

★**Date created**: The falls started to form about 12,000 years ago and continue today

★**Size**: **Horseshoe Falls** 2,220 ft (670 m) wide, **American Falls** 850 ft (260 m) wide, and **Bridal Veil** Fall 50 ft (15 m) wide. Their heights range from 65-190 ft (20-58 m) from the tops of the waterfalls to the river below

★**Water volume**: About 2,727,000,000 gallons (10,322,813,070 liters) per hour (about 4,131 Olympic-sized swimming pools)

★Niagara Falls has three different waterfalls: Horseshoe Falls (also known as the Canadian Falls), American Falls, and Bridal Veil Falls.

★The waterfalls get their water now from 4 of the 5 Great Lakes: Lake Huron, Lake Superior, Lake Michigan, and Lake Erie. Then Niagara Falls flows into the 5th Great Lakes, Lake Ontario.

★There is a small island named Luna Island separates the American Falls and Bridal Veil Falls, and you can get there by crossing a bridge on foot. This island got its name from the "lunar rainbows" it can create at night during a full moon.

Learning About the World Around Us!

★The falls have never been frozen solid, even though they will look like it. When the temperatures get cold enough, the top layer of the falls will freeze over, but the water underneath keeps flowing.

★The Falls can make 4 million kilowatts of electricity, supplying more than a quarter of all the power used in New York State, the USA, and Ontario, Canada.

★People have gone over the falls and lived! The first person to go over Niagara Falls in a barrel was 63-year-old school teacher Annie Edson Taylor.

★You can take a boat tour at the bottom of the falls to get an up-close view, but bring a raincoat because you will get wet.

★Nine people have tightrope walked across the falls. The first walk was in 1859 by a French man named Jean Francois Gravelet. Only one person died out of the nine people who walked across the falls.

American Falls and the Bridal Veil Falls

Horseshoe Falls

The falls almost froze in 1911

The Great Blondin carrying his manager in 1859

......**Annie Edson Taylor 1901**......

Where learning language online is fun!

Learning About the World Around Us!

Old Faithful Geyser

★<u>Location</u>: **Yellowstone National Park, Wyoming, U.S.A. (Continent of North America)**

★<u>Built by:</u> There is a supervolcano under the park at Yellowstone. The volcano heats underground water, and when there is too much pressure, it causes the water to erupt.

★<u>Date created</u>: About 15,000 years ago

★<u>Size</u>: It shoots water 130-140 ft (39-42 m) into the air

★<u>Water volume</u>: It sprays about 3,700-8,400 gal (14,006-32,000 L) at a time (about 3,700-8,400 plastic gal (L) of milk)

★The water that comes out is about 204° F (96 C), and the steam is about 350° F (178 C).

★It erupts every 91 minutes on average, about 20 times daily, lasting between 1.5-5 minutes.

★This volcano erupted three times; the last time was about 640,000 years ago. Scientists believe there will not be another eruption for another 100,000 years, but there will be global devastation when it does happen. 1 in - 4 ft (3 cm-1.5 m) of thick poisonous ash would cover hundreds of miles (kilometers) in the Northwestern part of the US and the Southern part of Canada. The ash will also lead to much colder weather and less crop production.

Learning About the World Around Us!

★Around the park, at Yellowstone, you can see many kinds of animals, like bison, wolves, bears (black and grizzlies), eagles (bald and golden), elk, moose, and moose many more. Do not feed these animals; you could get a $5,000 fine and maybe even prison time.

★There are trails throughout the area where you can hike. There are other lesser-known geysers, and you can fish in nearby lakes.

★Old Faithful was named in 1870 by Henry Washburn, who was on an expedition to explore the western territory of the US. He noticed the eruption's consistency and named it "Old Faithful." Before the current name, the Native American tribes had different names; the Crow Tribe called it "The land of burning ground," and the Blackfeet called it "The place of hot water." Each tribe also had multiple names, which depended on which area the tribe members lived in.

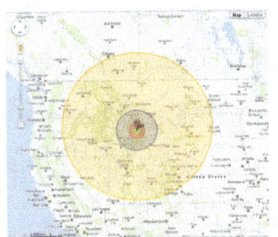
Yellowstone eruption zone

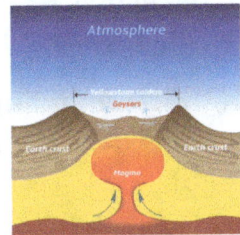
Magma chamber drawing

One of many smaller hot springs

Mammoth Hot Springs

Buffalo

Deer

Fox

Learning About the World Around Us!

Petra

★**Location**: **Jordan (Continent of Asia and in the Middle East region)**

★**Built by:** Nabataeans (an old civilization in this region)

★**How long to build**: Between 312 BC to about 110 AD (about 400 years), the people of Petra were continuously craving buildings, tombs, homes, and much more in the mountains in the area.

★**Date built**: Building started in 312 BC, and the city is half-built and half-carved out of the rocks from the surrounding mountains (about 2300 years ago)

★**Size**: About 23 sq m (60 sq km) area and some of the buildings are about 131 ft (40 m) tall, and some are even bigger

★Petra gets its name from the Greek word "Petros," which means "rocks," and it is also called the "Rose City" because of the pink color of the sandstone at sunset and sunrise.

★It was the capital city of the Nabataean civilization and an important trade city where they would trade silks, enslaved people, ceramics, and spice.

★Even though the city was in the desert, it had enough water for its 20,000 – 30,000 residents because it had a man-made water system made with terra cotta pipes throughout the city.

Learning About the World Around Us!

★Around 110 AD, the Romans had taken over the city; in 363 AD, a major earthquake destroyed half the city. By 700 AD, only a small group lived in the city.

★It was hidden from outsiders for hundreds of years before Swiss explorer Johann Ludwig Burckhardt rediscovered it in 1812. He disguised himself as a local Bedouin (the people who live in this area), could enter the city unnoticed, and noted what he saw.

★Only about 15% of Petra has been discovered.

★Archaeologists have found around 1,000 tombs carved throughout Petra, and they have painted decorations with pictures of what the person did in their life.

★One of the most famous buildings in the city is called the "Treasury," It got its name because it looked like a bank and held the city's money. It was a tomb for the royal families. Under the floor of the building, archeologists found three rooms and skeletal remains.

Learning About the World Around Us!

The Sphinx

★**Location**: **Giza, Egypt** **(Continent of Africa)**

★**Built by:** Archaeologists believe the construction was during the reign of the Pharaoh Khafre, but they are still looking for more evidence to support this idea

★**How long to build**: Archaeologists think it took about three years to build

★**Date built**: Between 2603-2578 BC (about 4,500 years ago)

★**Size**: It is 240 ft (73 m) long and 66 ft (20 m) high and was carved out of a single piece of limestone

★**Weight**: 40,000 lbs (18,000 kg) (about 10 African elephants)

★The colossal limestone statue of a creature with a lion's body and a human's head. He is a mythological figure in Egyptian, Asian, and Greek mythology (old stories that helped explain natural or traditional events in a culture).

★It is a spiritual guardian for the pharaoh, and archaeologists found many smaller statues at different sites around Egypt.

★Pharaoh Khafre's father was Pharaoh Khufu, who built the Great Pyramid behind the Sphinx.

Learning About the World Around Us!

★Archaeologists found paint residue (small pieces of paint) on the statue, so they think it was once painted red, with some parts also having blue and yellow paint.

★No one knows what happened to its nose, but many theories exist. One theory is that it broke off during a war with Napoleon Bonaparte. Another idea is that a man from another religion destroyed it in the name of his religion. Other people think it might have fallen off naturally due to the weather.

★There also used to be a beard, but it broke off due to erosion. In a museum in England, you can find some of the pieces. Archaeologists believe Egyptians may have added the beard after earlier Egyptians built the original statue.

★Much like the Great Pyramid, the Egyptians took excellent care of the workers of The Sphinx. Archaeologists have found the remains of what workers used to eat near the site. People with less money would eat more fish, beans, and vegetables.

★After some years, the people in this area decided to leave and left the statue uncared for. Over time, the statue was covered up to the head with sand. It wasn't until the 1930s that the Sphinx was fully unburied.

Picture taken around the 1930s

Learning About the World Around Us!

The Statue of Liberty

★**Location**: **Liberty Island in New York Harbor, New York, NY U.S.A.** (Continent of North America)

★**Built by:** French sculptor Frédéric Auguste Bartholdi and built by Gustave Eiffel

★**Date built**: The unveiling was on October 28, 1886, and the statue was called "Liberty Enlightening the World" ("The Statue of Liberty" is a nickname) (almost 140 years ago)

★**How long to build**: It took about eight years to build and about four months to put back together

★**Size**: It is 305 ft (93 m) tall

★**Weight**: 450,000 lb (225 tons)

★This monument would honor the United State's centennial of independence (100 years of freedom from England) and its friendship with France.

★Bartholdi came to America and spotted the current island it sits on now. Bartholdi thought this spot was the "Gateway to America." He wanted the statue to welcome immigrants (people coming from another country) and visitors as they sailed into the harbor.

★It was built in France but put together in America. When the statue arrived in America, the workers failed to complete the base of the statue, and they assembled it almost a year later.

Learning About the World Around Us!

★When they brought the statue over, it was in 350 pieces and took about four months to assemble once it got to America.

★There are 7 points on her crown representing the world's seven continents; each point is about 9 ft (3 m) long.

★Her tablet reads July IV, MDCCLXXVI (July 4th, 1776, the day America gained independence).

★On her feet, she has chains representing her freedom from oppression (unfair treatment).

★You can take tours of the island where she stands and go up into her crown.

★It is made out of copper. Why is it a greenish color now??

Stairs leading to the crown.

Statue of Liberty under construction in France.

Her head on display in a French park before coming to America.

Where learning language online is fun!

Learning About the World Around Us!

Stonehenge

★<u>Location</u>: Salisbury Plain, Wiltshire, England (Continent of Europe)

★<u>Built by:</u> Archeologists don't know who built Stonehenge, but they believe local tribes worked together to build the massive monument. They left no written records of events during this time, so the site is a mystery.

★<u>Date built</u>: 2,000-2,500 BC (4,500 years ago in the late Neolithic Age)

★<u>How long to build</u>: It took about 1,500 years in 4 stages. The last stage was during the Bronze Age (1,500 BC)

★<u>Size</u>: About 330 ft (101 m) in diameter

★<u>Weight</u>: There are two types of stone at Stonehenge:

    -The outer stones are sarsen stones, a type of silcrete (quartz and cement mixture) weighing 25 tons (23 metric tons) each.
    -The inner stones are bluestones made from spotted dolerite (a type of quartz and other minerals mixture) weighing 2-5 tons (2-4.5 metric tons) each.

★It is a massive man-made prehistoric monument circle of standing stones.

★There were roughly 100 massive upright stones initially placed in a circular layout. There are only 38 still standing.

★The bluestones were brought from over 160 mi (257 km) away from the south in Wales. The sarsen stones were brought down some 20 mi (32 km) from the north in northern England.

Learning About the World Around Us!

★The stones have unusual sounds when an object hits them. They produce a loud clanging sound. Many people also think these stones have healing properties.

★Archeologists know it served as a cemetery in its earliest days and have found bone fragments and the remains of about 62 men, women, and children.

★Stonehenge is aligned with the sunset of the Winter Solstice (the start of winter) and the sunrise of the Summer Solstice (the start of summer). Today and throughout history, many people gather here on these days to celebrate the start of the new season.

★There is some evidence now that the site performed as a calendar. The outer ring was to keep track of the months and days, and they would know the days and months by when the sun was shining in the circle. They had other stones inside the circle that accounted for Leap Year and five additional days in their calendar.

★There is a legend that a famous wizard named Merlin magically moved the massive stones from Ireland to England after fighting a battle against invading Saxtons. He moved it here to symbolize the Britons who had died in the battle. Merlin also helps the legendary King Author and the Knights of the Round Table.

Spotted dolerite **Sarsen stones**

Summer Solstice (sunrise)   **Winter Solstice (sunset)**

Learning About the World Around Us!

The Taj Mahal

★<u>Location</u>: **Agra, India (Continent of Asia)**

★<u>Date built</u>: It was built in 1632 (about 390 years ago)

★<u>Built by:</u> Mughal Emperor Shah Jahan as a mausoleum (tomb) for his beloved wife Mumtaz Mahal, who died in childbirth (their 14th child!)

★<u>How long to build</u>: In total, it took 22 years to build the whole complex where the Taj Mahal sits

★<u>Size</u>: 240 ft (73 m) tall & the complex in total is about 42 acres (17 hectares) or 20 soccer fields

★<u>Weight</u>: About 70,000-100,000 tons (10 million kg)

★The tomb houses the bodies of Mumtaz Mahal and Shah Jahan in a secret, quiet room under the main room.

★The mausoleum is made of white marble with semi-precious stones (including jade, crystal, amethyst, and turquoise), forming detailed designs.

★It is designed with Persian, Islamic, and Indian influences throughout the complex.

★The complex and building are almost symmetrical (similar parts facing each other).

Learning About the World Around Us!

★During different times of the day, the Taj Mahal will look different colors because of its materials and the sun's position.

★Over 20,000 workers and some 1,000 elephants helped build the mausoleum complex. The workers who worked on the structure were fed and treated very well.

★Also, the complex has two other buildings: a mosque (a Muslim church) and a guest house.

★The four towers were built slightly leaning forward, and they did this for two reasons: in case of an earthquake, they would not fall on the building, and when you first enter the complex, it makes the Taj Mahal seem bigger.

.......Mosque.......

The tomb of Emperor Shah Jahan (taller tomb) and his wife (shorter tomb)

Where learning language online is fun!

Learning About the World Around Us!

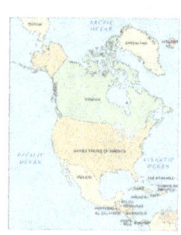

The Temple of the Great Jaguar Tikal

★**Location**: **Tikal, Guatemala (Continent of North America and in the region of Central America)**

★**Built by:** The Maya built it for their ruler Jasaw Chan K'awiil I after his death for his tomb

★**How long to build**: About 32 years

★**Date built**: Around 732 A.D (about 1,300 years ago)

★**Size**: The temple is over 155 ft (47 m) tall, with nine tiers (levels) representing the nine levels of the underworld (the place you go after you die, for the Maya) making up the temple.

★After Jasaw died, his burial chamber was the first room to be made, and then the temple was built around it, with Jasaw carved on the top of the temple, sitting on a jaguar throne. When archaeologists entered the chamber, they found jade figures and jewelry, pearls, jaguar furs, rare shells, jugs, mirrors, and even human bones with other loyal leader's names on them and his enemy's names.

★The city of Tika was the capital and most powerful city of the Maya, and there were royal palaces, residential homes, schools, hospitals, shops and markets, sports arenas (they played a game like basketball), and other smaller temples, with over 3,000 buildings throughout the city.

★ The Maya Civilization ruled here and was one of the most influential cities from 200 to 900 A.D (about 1,800-1,100 years ago).

Learning About the World Around Us!

★There was a population of about 25,000 at its low point and as high as 100,000 people during its peak.

★The Mayans are known for their calendar making, architecture, chocolate, rubber, and their study of astronomy (study of the stars), and they were terrific farmers.

★Historians think the Mayan empire collapsed because of war, overpopulation, drought, and illness.

View from the top of the jungle.

Mayan carving.

One of many temples.

Where learning language online is fun!

Learning About the World Around Us!

The Uyuni Salt Flat

★**Location**: **Southern Bolivia (Continent of South America)**

★**Created by:** Created after the prehistoric salt lake Lago Machín dried up

★**Date created**: 25,000 to 10,000 years ago

★**Size**: It is about 4,050 sq mi (10,489 sq km) in size

★**Weight**: It contains roughly 12 billion tons (10 billion metric tons) of salt

★It is the world's largest salt flat and the flattest area of land on Earth.

★When the area gets a little rain, it makes the salt flat look like a mirror

★GPS satellite companies will calibrate their satellites on the reflection when the salt flat has a mirrored look from the rain. These companies would typically use the ocean to help with their satellites.

★Part of the salt flat can be about 30 ft (9 m) thick.

★The towns surrounding do mine the salt flat for its salt, and you can buy it at local supermarkets.

★There is also lithium (a type of metal used for batteries) under the top layer of salt. Geologists estimate that about 30%-60% of the world's supply is here.

★When this area was a lake, evidence showed that snails, algae, mollusks, and microanimals once lived there.

Where learning language online is fun!

Learning About the World Around Us!

★There are about 35 islands throughout the area. The most famous island is called Isla Incahuasi. Isla Inchuasi has cacti and coral fossils that are thousands of years old. You can also take a tour of the island.

★There is also an abandoned train graveyard. This graveyard is where hundreds of old trains and carriages go after they are no longer useable. You can climb on the trains, and there is even a swing.

★Right on the edge of the salt flats is a hotel constructed of salt. You can rent a room here and get guided tours of the flats.

One of many islands throughout the salt flat.

Luna Salada Hotel de Sal

Train graveyard

Learning About the World Around Us!

Victoria Falls

★<u>Location</u>: **On the border of Zambia and Zimbabwe in Africa (Continent of Africa)**

★<u>Created by:</u> Around 100 million years ago, many small volcanic eruptions in this area caused cracks in the rocks and lava to cool and settle at the bottom. The Earth's movement of the 2 African tectonic plates also helped form the crack in the rock (no waterfall yet). About 10 million years ago, there was a massive flood in this area, which rerouted rivers and created the waterfall

★<u>Date created</u>: 10 million-100 million years ago

★<u>Size:</u> It is the largest waterfall in the world, 360 ft (108 m) tall & 5,605 ft (1,708 m) wide

★<u>Water volume</u>: 132 million g (500 million l) of water goes over the fall every minute, which is about 200 Olympic swimming pools

★North-Western Zimbabwe has a rainforest growing because of the water spray from the waterfall.

★Initially called "Mosi-oa-tuna," which means "The Smoke That Thunders," in 1855, it was named after Queen Victoria by explorer and missionary David Livingstone. He was the first European to have documented the falls.

★The falls are a part of the Zambezi River, the 4th largest river in Africa, 1,677 mi (2,700 km).

Learning LOL

Where learning language online is fun!

Learning About the World Around Us!

★When there is a full moon and the sunset, something rare happens: a "Moonbow," a rainbow at night.

★There is a part of the falls called "The Devil's Pool," where you can swim to the waterfall's edge and look over. You must be with a proper guide for this and be super careful!

★There are many different animals in the surrounding national parks: warthogs, elephants, lions, leopards, baboons, hyenas, zebras, and so many more.

"The Devil's Pool"

Moonbow

A bridge connecting Zambian and Zimbabwe

Baboon

Hyenas

Warthog

Leopard

The Zhangjiajie Glass Bridge

★<u>**Location**</u>: **Zhangjiajie, Hunan, China (Continent of Asia)**

★<u>**Built by:**</u> Designed by Israeli Architect Haim Dotan

★<u>**How long to build**</u>: About 18 months

★<u>**Date built**</u>: Construction completed in 2016

★<u>**Size:**</u> It is 1,410 ft (430 m) long, 20 ft (6 m) wide, 984 ft (300 m) high

★<u>**Weight:**</u> About 5 million lbs (2,200 tons)

★It is the world's longest and highest glass-bottomed bridge, and it is over the Zhangjiajie Grand Canyon (张家界大峡谷).

★There was a naming contest for the bridge, and the winner won $5,000 (¥30,000). The winning name was "Yun Tian Du" (云天渡), which means "the way for people under heaven."

★The bridge's design was to be as invisible as possible, to disappear into the clouds. This way, the natural beauty of the canyon could be seen.

★There are five layers of special glass and materials measuring about 2 in (50 mm) thick to help make up the bridge.

★To test the glass's strength, some invited visitors hit the glass with sledgehammers (massive hammers). It did break, but not into pieces because of the unique materials. (Don't worry; everyone was okay!) The designers proved their glass was strong by driving an SUV over the glass, and it did not break!

Learning About the World Around Us!

★It can hold up to 800 people at a time.

★There is a place where you can bungee jump 919 ft (280 m) into the canyon (the world's highest bungee jump), go ziplining, do yoga, and at night there is sometimes live entertainment like dancing, music, and fashion shows.

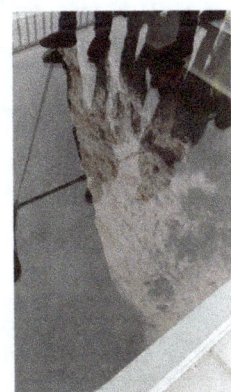

Where learning language online is fun!

Learning About the World Around Us!

Don't forget to check out our other books, Daily Vocabulary Worksheets Volume 1 and 2 & Daily Vocabulary Flashcards Volume 1 and 2.

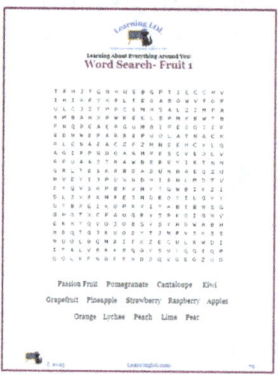

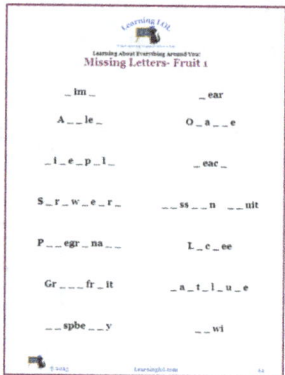

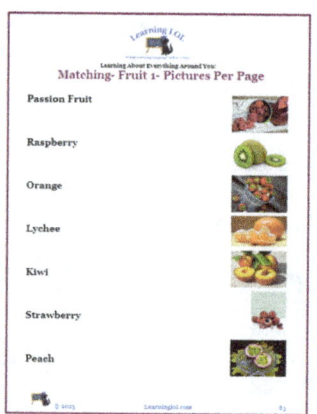

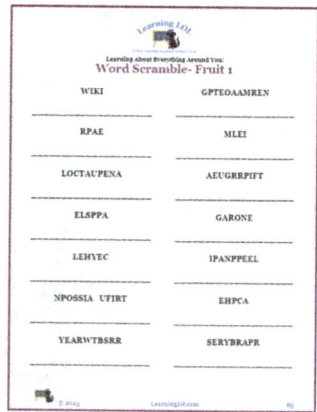

Where learning language online is fun!

Learning About the World Around Us!

Learning About the World Around Us!